THE
PATH
TO THE
Consciousness
OF Christ:

A Beginners Guide to Beginning

Sarah Reynolds

BALBOA.PRESS

A DIVISION OF HAY HOUSE

Balboa Press books may be ordered through booksellers or by contacting:

Balboa Press
A Division of Hay House
1663 Liberty Drive
Bloomington, IN 47403
www.balboapress.com
844-682-1282

Print information available on the last page.

ISBN: 978-1-9822-6366-9 (sc)
ISBN: 978-1-9822-6367-6 (e)

Balboa Press rev. date: 02/08/2021

This book is beautifully dedicated to Abigail, Sidney, Braxton, and Shelby Reynolds. Without you I would have never seen all the improvements that needed to be made on this Earth. I am forever grateful to get to be the one lighting up the path for you to follow.

It is important to me to give credit and appreciation where it is due. I could not have completed the book without my amazing editor, my great tribe cheering me on, those who inspired me to write the contents and those who helped me find my light in the darkness.

Before going a moment further, I would like to say how Christ's Consciousness has absolutely nothing to do with what religion you currently find yourself relating to. In fact, we would like to mention how in knowing and having a better knowledge of what the Christ's Consciousness is, you may find your religion more fun and appealing to you.

However, this book may have found its way to you due to the larger fact of how you are more spiritual than religious. This book will serve more as a guide to those of you who need it, no matter the religion, for your spiritual awakening and how to navigate it better mixed with a few of my own fun personal experiences.

Contents

Chapter 1

"Noone ever said it would be easy,
They said it would be worth it."

I have been walking around for as long as I can remember using the quote above as what some would call my "mantra". I have always found it to be inspiring in the most challenging of times. It is worthy to note that the journey to Christ's Consciousness is much like that quote. With coming into Consciousness, you will learn a lot of hard truths about mostly yourself but also the outside world. I've never been known to sugar coat the truth, so I didn't plan on starting that now.

So, let's get right down to business shall we? What is the Consciousness of Christ? In learning I find that the first easy step is to find a definition. The term "Christ" means a person who is conscious of their behavior and actions. A person who can give/receive love and compassion without wanting anything back in return. "Christ's Consciousness" means a person who embraces and demonstrates divinity. Divinity refers to the highest characteristics, personal qualities of the absolute divine. Therefore, a "Divine Person" means an individual that can demonstrate and project the attributes of unconditional love and compassion consciously through their thoughts, actions, and behaviors. "Christ" also refers to the awareness of the divinity and your primary purpose as a spiritual being. When you have found your spiritual connection with the Universe and with the creator, this will manifest outwardly as unconditional love, joy, and compassion. When an individual consciously demonstrates these divine attributes this is known as "Christ Consciousness". When we speak about the second coming of Jesus, often what we are actually referring to is we will all return back to the vibration of God source. The frequency associated with the Absolute Divine; Christ's Consciousness.

When a person is willing to learn and apply the principles of divinity in their life, they have spiritually evolved. Divinity helps you outwardly perceive the love and compassion in others. You recognize that each person is a spiritual being and understand that each person is at a different level of spiritual growth. When you integrate divinity as an internal part of yourself, you begin to externalize this Christ's energy. Christ energy only requires you to be open to a new way of living and your willingness to learn, integrate, and practice divinity on Earth. The important thing to keep in mind is your own ascension journey. You only need your conscious intent and genuine desires towards wanting to experience a world that operates on unity, love, and compassion which will help all of us achieve Christ energy.

Christ consciousness can include your ability to connect to your higher self, how to demonstrate the qualities of divinity and your ability to share your spiritual wisdom and knowledge to help others with their spiritual growth. A person who has activated the upper Chakras: the heart, third eye, and the crown have achieved "Christ Consciousness" because the process shifts a person's frequency into the powerful heart based qualities which allows them to consciously demonstrate love, empathy, compassion, and gives them ability to connect and understand people from a deeper emotional and spiritual level. These people can also have the ability to telepathically communicate with guides and the angelic realm.

Seems like a rather large task to accomplish in a day right? That's because the part no one wants to talk about is how hard all this actually is. Most assume if it is not love, light, and happiness then they are somehow doing it wrong. Everyone's experience is different. We all learn differently, feel differently, comprehend differently, and see differently, and once you come into understanding the work you have done and the progress you have made, you simply never want to recollect and share all the steps they went through to become who they are.

Oftentimes, I assure you, this path of alignment feels rather unfair and alone. Most people have become so unoriginal that they simply do not know what they even really enjoy anymore. They do not know what is best for them. They do not know what truly makes their hearts and souls happy. But mostly they all know exactly what they do not like, and they want to complain to every single soul about all of those things. So, by the end of your awakening you feel like a giant dried out, crumply, ole snake skin! Ha! Ok, maybe that is a bit dramatic, but times really do get rough as you start to see your realities more clearly. Just know, everything you have ever wanted really is right within your reach.

I'd find it honorable to mention merely for your spiritual understanding, if I have already gone over things or as topics and terms come up, if you feel a "spark" inside of you, Write those things down and learn about them. Explore them. That is your spirit responding with an eagerness to learn about the topics I am speaking about. We have also created a small glossary in the back to further help you along. I will go in detail with a few along the following pages including my personal experiences as well. Although I am not here to go into the full teachings of Christ consciousness, I merely wanted to give you a simple beginner's guide to your spiritual path unfolding and how you can help yourself. Because, after all, no one can do this type of self healing work, but you. No one can actually tell you how long your spiritual awakening will take. However, i've found journaling is a great way to keep track of yourself and your experiences.

So what exactly are the "steps to awakening"? I am sure more than a few are wondering. So, here we go! Step 1. The point of no return. As soon as you take your first step, whether it was something prior to this that led you to this book, or it could simply be this book found its way to you and is only the beginning. You are already past the point of no return. Even if you want to change your mind there simply is zero going back at this point. Step 2. Awakening, which is messy. Since awakening requires that we move from unconscious to Consciousness in all areas of life, specific issues will naturally arise in order to show you where you are asleep, and oftentimes, this can feel like, "Shit is hitting the fan.". Life issues will point out the prevalence of unconscious behaviors, especially those behaviors that are used to gain approval or acceptance from others. No matter how messy awakening may be, you can always count on the truth to clean up the mess.

Step 3, a complete internal overhaul. Although everyone's path is unique, no one awakens until they let go of the constructs and beliefs that have kept them asleep or on auto pilot. Therefore, somewhere on the path of awakening, you will need courage and willingness to examine and reexamine everything you once believed to be true, including age-old traditions, cultured beliefs, religious doctrines and even the beliefs and values that have formed the foundation of your life. Consequently when you begin to see through all the illusions that have been constructed by systems, religions, traditions, and so forth, you may question everything, and you might even come to the conclusion that all beliefs are false. No doubt, as you dissemble the construct of reality, you will likely find yourself on extremely shakey ground.

Step 4. Resistance is futile. Yes, you have free will to resist the process of awakening at any point. However, whether you like it or not, once you begin the journey, life circumstances will relentlessly push you towards awakening. So, not only is resistance futile, the more you resist, the more difficult your life becomes. Therefore, it is highly suggested to wave your flag and surrender as much as possible. The universe is conspiring your awakening. Surrender does not mean giving up or losing the battle. In fact everytime you surrender to a higher power, you'll be one step closer to awakening.

Step 5. The emotional roller coaster. Make absolutely no mistake, walking the path of awakening can be like a roller coaster ride. Like clockwork, unhealed past traumas and emotional wounds that have been stuffed or denied now will come up to clear, and oftentimes, issues you thought to be healed long ago resurfaced as well.

Step 6. Alienated friends and family. As you begin to raise your consciousness and awaken, you may discover that you no longer have anything in common with your friends and family. Due to your scrutiny and rejection of previous shared beliefs, that old familiar connection could be gone. No doubt, (from personal experiences),if you're alienated from the ones you love the most, it's common to feel lost and alone. Moreover, if your loved ones no longer understand you, they will claim your bat shit crazy, and off your rocker!

Stage 7. The anti-social phenomenon. During the process of awakening; small talk, and socializing often become quiet unappealing and even down right unbearable at times. So, although you might feel uneasy to spend large amounts of time alone, there's a good chance that, on most days, you'll choose it over small talk and socializing.

Step 8. The end of toleration. By stage 3 of the awakening process, it's very common to become hyper aware of unfulfilling relationships and/or careers that you have been quietly tolerating for years, and while this could prompt a growing desire for change, it's often followed by a debilitating fear of the unknown. Nonetheless, it's impossible to fully awaken while you continue to engage in circumstances where you are unconscious and asleep. Therefore, sooner or later, it's time to acknowledge your personal truths and make the changes necessary. So, let's be honest here, this does mean leaving behind unhealthy professional dynamics, and/or dysfunctional relationships. It could also mean setting and enforcing boundaries that support a more conscious life.

Step 9. Unrecognizable to yourself. As a result of questioning your own identity, at some point, you might realize that you are no longer the person you once believed yourself to be, and as you become unrecognizable to yourself, you may experience big life changes in a relationship, career, or physical relocation. Since the stranger in the mirror is more than likely you, it's a good idea to make friends with yourself. However, do your best not to judge or abandon your old self who did all the hard work to get you there.

Step 10. Letting Go. As the most pivotal factor, awakening requires a complete letting go, such as letting go of external judgements, self judgment, social systems, ego-generated behavior, emotional wounds, social, religious, and family beliefs, and even who you once thought you were. While this often is described as the "ego death", it's common to experience deep feelings of emptiness.

Step 11. Embracing the dark side. As an often hidden aspect of awakening, you must eventually face and embrace your dark side. Needless to say, if you're attached to the identity of being a good person, this can and will be a difficult phase. While it's easier to categorize people as good or bad and rationalize that you fall into the former category, we all contain aspects of light and dark, therefore we all have the ability to demonstrate both the best and worst of human-kind. Since awakening requires a return to wholeness, along with a high level of unconditional self-love and acceptance, your whole being must be integrated, even though parts of you, you dislike and strive to change. So, keep in mind as long as you don't hurt yourself or anyone else, it's ok to be friends with your inner "bad guy".

Step 12. Physical Symptoms. Let's not forget that during the process of awakening, vibrational changes in the body and psyche can cause all types of odd physical symptoms. My personal favorite (not) was the, "liquid fire", (as I call it) that felt to be burning through my body and blasting out, let's be real here, both my main openings to expel nasty business. So, before you fall off the deep end keep in mind that a variety of awakening symptoms are perfectly normal such as interrupted sleep, change in appetite, loss of desire, confusion, lightheadedness, bodily aches, pains, depression and more. (But of course, seek professional medical care when appropriate)

Step 13. Cycles of ups and downs. On this crazy and chaotic path of awakening, you'll likely have days when you feel on top of the world and you will think you finally "made it" …. Only to be shoved back down to the pits of confusion and despair the very next day. Since the cycle is pretty normal, why not enjoy the good days while doing your best to smooth out the bad ones? Thankfully, over time, the ups and downs will even out, and eventually, you'll discover a beautiful space to call home.

Step 14. What's the point? For most, the process of awakening often reveals that life has no real meaning or purpose, and this can result in a feeling of hopelessness and depression. After all, if there's no point to life, what's the point? However, rather than it being the end of the story, the best part of life begins after you move through the period of pointlessness. In fact, this is when you have the ability to consciously write your own life story, the way you always wanted it to be.

Step 15. Running out of time. If you're like many others on the path, you might experience pangs of regret for not starting the journey sooner, and you might even feel like you're running out of time. Rest assured, thanks to your inner clock, everyone begins to wake up at exactly the right time. Specific to THEM. Every life experience has propelled you toward awakening, and this means that there hasn't been a single wasted moment. So, try not to beat yourself up about it.

If you are new to being spiritually "woke" then I'm sure more of what is written here is probably terrifying. As I have stated above, no one can tell you what to do, how to help, etc as you are the only one going through this process. But now that I have outlined a few of the major identifiers of your transition, we can move forward and discuss the best parts to come from your spiritual awakening.

Chapter 2

Joy is the key! -Ester Hicks

✥

So, the first chapter of this book can feel like a daunting task to most. A lot of people will feel as if they are truly dying. I felt this so many times, So what we want to say here is this "Love and Light" feeling or phrase people claim to have felt, does not come until you have completed your own soul work. This is also phrased or called "Shadow work", "The Dark Night" or "Working on yourself". That does NOT mean that there will be zero good days in time of falling apart. Some days your angels, spirit guides, or spiritual team will orchestrate something so fantastic just for you! You will simply know and feel on your inside it was. And so many people would say, "Sarah, how do you know this to be true?" As I have walked around mainly "open" my entire life, I've had a lot of time to simply absorb the energy. Which is never a sufficient answer for most people. So, simply when you see, hear, smell, touch, and feel something and your body reacts to the knowledge you can feel a tingling, light up, spark sensation inside of you. That is a piece of your soul waking up and responding, "Hey! That's us!"

I mention this in great detail as it is truly important for you to rebuild a relationship with yourself in order to develop a relationship with your higher self to obtain the consciousness of Christ.

So, now you say "Great, thank you for identifying step one. But how do I get to know myself?" For myself and mostly everyone who has done soul work, we will say, "Oh man, self care is the key." But, in today's society I learned 1. Everyone's idea and version of self care is different. Simply because it leads us all to different things we enjoy. 2. In the current culture this phrase has been so ….. misunderstood. People honestly struggle to know what self care is or how to do it. After doing my own soul work and coming into understanding of myself and my purpose, I learned, I was probably actually really qualified to show the world how to unconditionally love themselves' and others. But, I do find it important to mention here, there was a lot of *muck* I had to go through to get right to where I am.

For a lot of people I believe they think "self-care" means "Personal Hygiene" as the markets have super dominated and coined this phrase. Sometimes, yes, I do enjoy a nice flowery salt bath with my favorite face mask. Yes, sometimes it may be a warm shower to cleanse my aura. Most people simply find water to be healing, it just is. Self care is about so much more than that though. Do me a favor real quick, simply ask yourself this question in your head, "Do I care about myself?" What did your heart say? Did you get a good feeling or a bad feeling? If you had no feeling, I'd say it's a safe bet, you do not. So now let me ask you this, "In what ways do you care for yourself?" Can you make a list? Do you like music? Do you like reading? Do you like to be outdoors? How can you do more of what you like or be better at what you already enjoy? The key here is to spark your interest in what you already do actually like. A really great way to start self care is to simply enjoy more of what you already like and see where the road takes you.

Really, to be perfectly clear we want you to understand this *inside self discovery* is really where the *magic* happens. Rediscovering yourself and who you truly are can be such an interesting and fun journey. While doing more of what you do like however, I assure you, you will be exposed to more of what you don't like. This is important for many numerous reasons that many people can explain. But for my intents and purposes of this book we will say "When you begin to see "so much" of what you don't like, it forces you to make better choices for yourself."

People struggle to clearly realize that this work requires you to let go of people, places, and things that no longer serve them. I will mention to you though, sometimes you do feel horrible for having to make these changes and stand up for yourself. But it is the most important thing that happens. Sometimes, you really do have to leave that job, leave that person,or make a move. Honestly, during this period you will "detox" yourself and your life. I use the word detox because if you have had a nasty habit, you will understand how fitting this is. It really isn't a fun process but you will love the end result that is you! I can already assure you, you will be exactly loved for being exactly who you are.

Once you feel like you've gotten good and comfortable doing and exploring the things you do like, it is important to not just excelle at those things, but then it is time to start digging deeper into who you really are, your past experiences, who you want to be, and who you were meant to be. Most will naturally come to these questions if they haven't already been asking any way. You will find the answers to those questions by digging deeper into yourself.

During much of the awakening/ascension process, you will still feel negative energy around you. I simply mention this because the darker entities of this realm simply do not want for you to wake up. They would rather hold you in bondage. So you will want to be mindful and not have your social media home screens filled with negative talk, fake news, or fake friends. You do not truly know everyone in this universe or their intentions. That's why you need to be connected to your higher consciousness.

During this shadow phase, while finding yourself alone and lonely, try to start meditation. And please, try to keep in mind that none of us are perfect. If you don't get it on the first try, keep trying. The negative forces in this universe *WANT* you to give up. They *NEED* you to be their slaves. It can only be up to you to not allow these negative forces in. Giving up is just never really the answer unfortunately.

You have an entire spiritual team just waiting to meet you! Filled with angels, ancestors, elementals, guardians, the list is simply endless and each one of them signed up to help you because they believe in you and they love you! Isn't that possibly the best news you've heard this week? I simply believe if you can do the work, simply because you believe you deserve to feel love unconditionally, you will find your way to the consciousness that is Christ. And when you do, you will see, know, and feel this love is exactly true.

Since a young age, maybe 12 or 13, I have always liked to study and know different cultures and religious teachings. As a child, I never really gave that much thought, other than I like to learn or know. As I have gotten older and, in doing my own soul work, I am constantly finding more and more hidden gems and lost knowledge that other people may or may not need to learn but, for certain, hold value and meaning for me. I woke one day to the term "gypsy" floating around in my "head space" … for myself, I guess you could say, I "see" "terms" in my mind. Usually ones that my guides need me to do some research on. Although, sometimes, I do not start my research instantly because I need to wait for further "intelligence" to know exactly where I need to start. So, while speaking with a friend in a super casual conversation he said to me "I always just assumed you knew we were gypsies, and that's why we move around a lot" In that moment I thought, well heck no! I did not know that! Had you mentioned this a long time ago it would have made sense. But later …. I considered, maybe this was true to a certain extent. Either way, I definitely needed to seek out some knowledge of gypsies.

So, we began our research. I go to the internet searcher, and merely want to see the gypsy deities. Would you know, I came across a "Patron Saint" of the Romani people? Saint Sarah. Which if you are a person who believes in coincidences, this may be one. However, I felt so elated to come across this information. I felt like I was seriously on my way to discovering *something*. I just wasn't really sure what that was yet. I found it heavily interesting that Sarah was actually not a Saint in the Catholic church and falls into a category of "Folk Christian". Have you ever heard of that classification? We hadn't either! I also read that in the book "Holy Blood, Holy Grail", It suggests that Sarah was the daughter of Jesus Christ and Mary Magdalene.

I will be the first to admit that, the hardest part of having an open mind, is being open to believing the information you are receiving. At first, I just thought it was so fun that I had stumbled onto the info that there was a Saint that shared a name with me. *tootes fake magical trumpet* Check and Done. "That was so fun to learn spirit guides, thank you!" *we all high five*

Before continuing with what I learned, I think it is indeed important for you to understand at this point, my already fallen apart life, that had already fallen apart a few times, took a really drastic turn for the worst, yet again. I got shoved out of my comfort zone. Which had been a vicious cycle for all of 3 years by this point but this specific incident led to my very own "ego death". I simply had to start doing what was best for me.

The next day after this lowest of low days, I woke up with a feeling that I could best describe to be the word or term, "raptured". There was the term, once again, floating around in my head space. I began to think "Why do you feel so elated, happy, joyus? The term "raptured" surely felt like a proper term compared to the day before." Honestly, I had felt like my angels had taken my body to the higher realms, healed me, and plopped me back into my Earthly body, and gave me a cup of coffee. I felt so strange. For 3 solid weeks, my attitude and spirit shared nothing but love and light. I felt so amazing. This is how I am supposed to be, I thought. Just happy, unconditionally loving everyone.

Unfortunately, I hadn't remembered the part, that it is hard to unconditionally love someone else when they do not unconditionally love themself. So, while trying to hold on to a relationship in which the other person did not unconditionally love themselves, I could feel the darkness lurking and hovering behind me.

After receiving days worth of light codes, I was encouraged by my spirit team to revisit my knowledge on "Saint Sarah". I had apparently missed something according to them. Some of you may ask how or why I have this knowledge. I would like to mention, I have always had a strong desire that leads me to figuring out myself, who I am, and where I come from. Many people do this daily without realizing it, for example, the phrase "Where my soul tribe at?" Please know, when you ask a question, the answer is given. It may require you to do a little work, but it is there.

When I went back to find the info again I finally saw it clearly. "Daughter of Jesus Christ and Mary Magdalene". My heart elated once more. I WAS the daughter of Jesus Christ! I knew it! I had accepted him in my heart years ago. It was then, I realized the love I was feeling was the Christ Consciousness coming through me.

Although I felt this to be true in my heart, I instantly knew what I needed to do next. Yup, you guessed. More work, I needed to know more about Jesus and Mary Magdalene's relationship. I simply had to.

In that, I found, it was Mary Magdalene who carried the energy and teachings of the Christ Consciousness into western Europe through France. When Mary Magdalena settled in France, she began the work of holding the Christ Light through her presence as part of the sacred Twin Flame energy, as well as sharing the energy of the message of the teachings of the Christ Consciousness. This basic meaning was peace, abundance, unconditional love, and the knowledge that a time would come when the Earth would be filled with a species of humans who would carry the Christ Consciousness, and who would manifest the Golden Age of Peace and Harmony.

In order to share the energy and teachings, Mary traveled extensively and worked as a teacher and leader. The heritage of feminine spiritual leadership and divine beauty that was her energy, still lingers in tradition and heritage of the troubadour, musicians, and poets.

Of course, after the Catholic Crusades and the inquisition, very little remained of this heritage and the stories of the "Holy Grail" are poorly received and understood by today's scholars. In its most simple form, this is the essence of what Mary Magdalena brought to France. She taught her understanding of the "Sacred" or "Twin Flame" union as a model for sacred union. Mary knew this form of "spiritual marriage" based on service of light, would become a pattern or template for relationships and union in the upcoming Golden age or New Earth.

Mary Magdalena also taught that the human body itself was "The Holy Grail", the vessel or container of the soul and spirit and the divine essence of God. When the consciousness within the sacred vessel of matter was in a sufficiently high vibration, then that matter would be transmuted into angelic light and the human being would become a human angel.

In Mary's teachings, every human was capable of raising their consciousness to the level where this angelic transmutation would be possible. But, she knew this would all take time. Mary Magdalena knew that there would be energies and forces that would work against the new evolution of Consciousness. However, she also knew her teachings and her energy would survive in this place, and that they would be carried out into the new world.

Mary knew this would be needed at this time of consciousness shift, for the masculine energy that was needed to populate the planet would have come to dominate to such an extent that it would be necessary to bring back the feminine energy and to create the balance needed to create the "Sacred Union", and to implement the golden grid of Twin Flame union that would hold the geometrical pattern for the Golden Energy of Twin Flame love.

For, the Christ's Consciousness as taught by Mary Magdalena is seated in the heart. It is the heart that carries the higher frequency of love, joy, and peace. It is only by opening the heart that we can achieve the Consciousness of the Grail within ourselves and then be ready to share that with others.

So, as this was all pretty mind blowing things to myself personally, in the moment it resonated so hard with the core of who I am, all I could simply say was "Well, these two obviously had an interesting relationship".

Days later, after finding this information, I found myself once again lost in conversation with a soul dear to me, where we began discussing the Christ Consciousness. I felt so moved, empowered, elated, I merely responded back "People really need to know about this, someone should write a book!"

And boy, let me tell you …. Did the bells, whistles, and alarms start going off inside my head! So I thought to myself, "How am I in any way qualified for this task?" I heard spirit say, "Because, no one can understand as clearly as you can Princess. This is your task, no one else." Talk about taboo, pressure, and stepping up to fulfill your soul's destiny! I was completely in!

By the way, yes, my guides do call me princess. The literal meaning of Sarah is princess. I too find that to be a fun little gift on top of so many others I have received.

I want you to understand, I did NOT write all of this to claim any sort of heritage by any means. I wrote all of this so you can clearly see the divine relationships you may be preventing yourself from having. I have more personal stories to share that I hope you will also find enlightening to help you on your journey.

Chapter 3

"The best way out is always
through" -Robert Frost

※

I would now like to discuss different types of spiritual tools
you can use during your transition. If you have already started
your spiritual journey most of these will not be new, but maybe
you will be able to figure out how they can be used for your own
purposes that maybe you didn't clearly see before.

The first major weapon in your tool box is boundaries. Some
of us are less perfect at boundaries than others. I learned this could
come from their souls true DNA and where it originates from. It
is up to you to set healthy boundaries for yourself. We know this
process isn't easy. Some people are extra persistent. Some are unaware
they are crossing a boundary and just need a little communication.
While others simply don't give a shit about your boundaries, and
they never will. The last group (spoiler alert) are usually the ones
you find yourself cutting ties with.

Regardless of how many times you have to do it, replace a new
heavier boundary between you and them until they are able to

respect you. I mean, let's be honest here, you are really great! You deserve nothing but the best and you shouldn't tolerate anything less than the best.

It's my opinion that no one ever really explained to some of us, sometimes it is hard doing what's best for you and breaking your own heart. So, I want you to know from me, yes, it does hurt. It is sad. But it's gonna be worth it.

When people "awaken" they naturally enjoy nature. Mother Earth in all her beautiful splendor seems to captivate you, as you hear the birds chirping for what feels like the first time. Our beautiful Mother Earth also holds the best tools for us. When things are collected naturally, they have a more refined connection to the Earth rather than ones handled and processed in shipping houses. It is during all this "handling" that other people are able to absorb the energy or leave traces of their own, on your product. How many people handled it before it got to you?

Plants are one of my MANY pleasures. Ha! My heart sang a little as I wrote that part. Ok, maybe I should just say, I LOVE *PLANTS*! But, if I told you how much I simply loved everything, that would be less than helpful. I love everything so much, in every way that, I want you to be able to love it too! Whew, I am so glad we got that out of the way!

I am a firm believer in having plants inside, outside, over here, and over there. I also suggest using plants that are dried out to spiritually cleanse your space. Some of the main plants great for that are Sage, Rosemary, Lavender, and mint. However the more you get to know plants the more you understand their purposes and how they can help you. Keeping a spiritually cleansed space to evolve in, is going to feel like your safe haven. Way more soothing than one filled with anger, rage, or sadness.

Our history dating back throughout time has so much history and knowledge of stones, gems, and minerals. Every culture has its own beliefs about specific stones, and those beliefs are often tied to that specific culture's history, geography, and spiritual practices. It should be of no surprise by now dear friend, that I also love to speak about stones.

What is also pleasing is you can educate yourself on stones, rocks, and gems on any social platform. And if you haven't made an Etsy account yet, there is an entire community of amazing souls out there who find nothing but pure joy in gathering your metaphysical needs. Please consider doing yourself a favor of ordering from a shop on there instead of a big box company.

But I am telling you, if you have the opportunity to go mining for your own gems, you should definitely try it. It is an enlightening experience to have all around. Life is full of adventures pal, don't forget to take yourself on one.

I can feel spirit getting tingly about this next part. "Well, everyone knows about rocks and plants!" They say. I like rocks and plants thank you. They are always an honorable mention. So, what I will tell you about next is meditation. "Ohhhh meditation, no one has ever heard of this" … sassy little spirit bunch I have aye? *laughing*

Once you become skilled in meditation, from your current point of standing, it is the easiest way to access the collective consciousness of all beings who have ever lived on the Earth. This is also known as The Akashic Records. Which is very interesting, if you happen to be into being able to access great knowledge. This magical database exists on the Astral plane, and contains infinite life experiences, as well as the keys to understanding the deeper Karmic Nature of all things in the universe.

Is your mind blown yet? It is believed that all the answers to all the questions can be found in the Akashic Records. Maybe you have heard of this before and maybe you haven't. Either way, this is powerful information to be shared.

For what seems like forever but we will say for *sometime* I have walked around thinking and saying "If you never know where you came from, how do you know which direction to go?" Most people never really understand this, even currently, as I write this.

I came across this beautiful soul named Cosmic Empress one night after going on one of my numerous quests for spirit. I knew she was in my energy field for a reason as soon as I witnessed her. Cosmic Empress had a message or "all call" for the Starseeds on YouTube. I won't ruin her message here, she says it all so much more beautiful than myself. But for me, the essence of the message was "You're almost there, finish waking up and come home".

Home? Oh man, she had me hooked. I had been searching for that place for what felt like 31 years already. After binge watching her channel for probably 2 hours, I had all the intel I needed.

Here is what I learned, my soul originates from the planet Hadar. Hadar is the planet of pure love! Imagine a place where every single thing simply loves you! The plants, the animals, the beings, the rocks, all of Hadar holds and emits love.

On this beautiful planet everyone communicated and interacted telepathically as there was never a need to hide anything from one another. When you love so unconditionally why would you ever need to hide something? Love is like breathing air for us. We will constantly be going out of our way to show our love for you. Sadly enough, even when that love isn't given back to us. We simply draw the conclusion that you just need more love, so we continue to give until we run out.

Hadarians are incredible "family" people. They emanate joy and love from their heart. You will notice people will simply gather around them and be so comforted by this person even if this person is paying them no attention.

Knowing this information would have saved me a ton of arguments in my 20s I believe. Having a partner who is "so comforted", is not always a blessing. Like I've mentioned, it is not all love and light.

These people also inspire others to have joy in their heart. Now, for me to know and understand all of this information was truly a gift for myself. But the real gift is knowing I am able to write this to help each of you begin or continue on your path of awakening and will someday feel the way I have.

We want to say, there are so many things that are not mentioned here that are spiritual tools. Candles, statues, paintings, we know the list goes on. Use tools you feel pulled and called to. There are so many beautiful souls who are out there waiting to meet you and help you on your journey. Find things that bring you joy and happiness. But really, you do not NEED any tools at all, everything you need, is already inside you.

Chapter 4

"Once you make a decision, the
Universe conspires to make it
happen" Ralph Waldo Emerson

❈

Before we get to the portion of how you can find your own answers, we find it necessary to say, "Once you know and understand the laws of the Universe, even if only in mild introduction or studied, you will be able to better navigate yourself in the Universe"

Which, I do find to be a good point because so many people are concerned with the laws of the land. They are so willing to obey so many rules and regulations that go against the very laws our world was created on. There are only 12 of these laws, which is an insanely low amount, considering how many are in your town, state, or Country. Can anyone think of why that may be?

The first is the Law of Divine Oneness. This law states we are all connected through creation. Which means every single thing you do has a ripple effect and impacts all of us collectively. All of humanity and God are one. We are always connected to the force of

God, because the energy of God is everywhere at once and permeates through all things living or material. Each soul is a part of God's energy.

The second is the Law of Vibration. Everything in the Universe has a frequency and vibration. Everything in the Universe moves, vibrates, and travels in circular patterns, the same principles of vibration in the physical world apply to our thoughts, feelings, desires, and wills in the Etheric world.

The third is the Law of Correspondence. The premise behind this law is that our lives are created by subconscious patterns we repeat every single day. These patterns either serve us or hold us back. Understand that there are multiple layers of our existence-mind, body, and spirit. This manifests on all planes and continues in an endless cycle. If you seek to change something about yourself, you must address the problem across all planes.

The fourth is the Law of Attraction. This is the law of vibration in action. For now, we will stay with the broad understanding that, whatever you do to others, will come back to you. Any word you speak to others or yourself, actions you take, thoughts you think, will come back in some form at some time. If you give out positive, although it is not immediate at times, the same vibration will be echoed back to you.

The fifth is the Law of Inspired Action. This law is about taking action in order to bring what you want into fruition. Also meaning, you are in alignment with yourself and who you want to be and from that position are taking the guided steps in your life to be who you want to be.

The sixth is the Law of Perpetual Transmutation of Energy. This law means that even the smallest action can have a profound effect.

As energy, we all have the power to change any conditions in our own lives. Producing a higher vibration consumes and transforms lower ones. This means we can change the energies in our lives by understanding the universal laws and applying them to produce change.

The seventh is the Law of Cause and Effect. Also known as the law of Karma. Which states that any action causes a reaction. In accordance to this law, every one of your thoughts, words, or actions sets a specific effect in motion which will come to materialize over time. Know that there is no luck or chance. They are simply terms used by humanity in ignorance of this law.

The eighth is the Law of Compensation. It's all about receiving compensation for all your contributions to the world around you including love, joy, and the kindness you spread. If you give freely without expectations then you will receive gifts, rewards, success, abundance, and monetary rewards more than you can imagine.

The ninth law is the Law of Relativity. Which sums up to be, nothing or no one is inherently good or bad. We are the ones who decide what is right or wrong. Each person will receive a series of problems for the purpose of strengthening the light within. Each of these lessons challenge us to remain connected to our hearts when proceeding to solve the problem. No matter how bad a situation is perceived, someone always has it worse. It's all relative.

The tenth law is the Law of Polarity. Simply meaning, if there is an up, there has to be a down. Light has darkness, joy has sorrow, and left has right.

The eleventh law is the Law of Rhythm. Everything vibrates and moves to certain rhythms. These rhythms establish seasons, cycles, stages of development, and patterns. Masters know how to rise above negative parts of a cycle by never getting excited or allowing negative things to enter their consciousness.

And finally, the twelfth law is the Law of Gender. Stating both masculine and feminine energies exist in all things. Masculine also means persistence and feminine meaning patient energy. You must find the balance between the both to manifest your desires.

We want to say here, once again, there are so many more souls way more advanced than myself in the areas of Universal Laws who you should turn to for further guidance and understanding of. Teaching you these specifics are their soul's purpose and they should be fully embraced for the hard work they do and continue to do for us on a collective level. We are sending you special souls who do this for us so much love for sharing yourselves, so we can better ourselves.

Chapter 5

"Synchronicity is an ever present
reality for those who have
eyes to see" -Carl Jung

———————— ❈ ————————

For the most part, becoming spiritually awakened leaves you asking a ton of questions and for some people that leads them down a path of losing faith and hope in higher beings. That is because they feel as if their prayers are not being answered. So, we want you to understand the real issue here is Free Will is always at play. You have every choice to not see, understand, or respond when your spirit team leaves you messages. So when you lose hope and faith it becomes counterproductive to your growth.

The negative forces in this world know and understand this well. So let me help you here by explaining a few different methods your spiritual team can use and how you can use your own.

In the spiritual community you will have several different people explain all different types of ways you can recieve your answers, naturally I have a few I would like to go over.

Tarot cards and oracle cards are great methods of receiving answers. The negative forces in this world have put judgement on these cards. They made so many believe they were an act of evil and predicted your future. Dear souls, we ask, how can that be so when our universe is run on free will? You can change the outcome of any situation with your choosing. The evil forces know if they keep you disconnected from your higher self, they can keep you in an oppressed state in order to keep you as their slave for longer. They need your soul in order to survive. Will you let them have it?

Tarot or Oracle cards simply are a tool that offers a way to focus your intuition so you can tune into spiritual guidance and insight. The cards themselves are not magic …. But rather they offer a mechanism for you to tune into the magic and divine guidance within yourself.

So a Tarot or Oracle spread is really a way in which you arrange the cards, after shuffling, to match the info you are seeking. I promise, it is not difficult. These spreads can range anywhere from 2 cards to 24. The spreads can offer you insight on mental healing, your past lives, if you can trust someone, and even how to better connect with your spirit guides. There are so many gifted artists designing these cards for us today. I always suggest getting the deck you feel is calling you to know it.

Numerology is any belief in the divine or mystical relationship between a number and one or more coinciding events. It is often associated with the paranormal alongside side astrology and other similar divination arts. Frequently people will report seeing the same numbers. Numbers on a clock, on a receipt, while working, or in everyday life.

When numbers keep coming at you, it's definitely a sign your spiritual guides are trying to reach out to you. Find the answers and decipher what they are telling you. The more you begin to understand and communicate with your guides, the easier your transition becomes. I find it helps me if I keep records which in case you couldn't gather, leaves me writing a whole bunch. I am never in short supply of pens and paper. It's worth me mentioning here, learning about yourself can become somewhat addictive, I also want to say it is the best thing you could ever become addicted to.

By using numerology, you are able to get better insight on yourself, the future, and the environment around you. Numerology can show you hidden meanings behind your own name, birth date, life path number, and show you your own destiny number.

Along your awakening you will also notice several synchronicities, such as finding random feathers or coins along your path that will come out of nowhere. Our guides can also use scents and clouds to reach out to us. I always find it incredibly sweet when my spiritual team plays songs for me on the radio. You will just instinctively *know* because it is referring to something in your life you are dealing with. All of these things come together and equal an answer or sign for you.

Your spirit guides may also be trying to communicate with you by vivid dreams and visions. They convey their messages through dreams and visions during meditation. By sharpening our senses, our spirit guides make us more observant to notice signals. Spirit guides often will deliver information and answers to us through our intuition.

Spiritual chills are something I experience almost daily. Frequent random chills throughout your body or sudden goosebumps happen when spirit is reaching out for you. Don't forget, signs from your guides could come in repeating numbers, animals, images, or even thoughts.

Sarah Reynolds

Some ways you can connect with your spirit guides and angels is by keeping your chakras clear, obtaining a daily meditation schedule, asking them to reveal themselves to you, or by asking them for a sign. My best advice always is, keep a spiritual journal.

Astrology is the study of movements and relative positions of celestial bodies interpreted as having an influence on human affairs and the natural world. One of the largely known parts of Astrology is horoscopes. Horoscopes forecast a person's future, typically including a delineation of character and circumstances. Based on the relative positions of the stars and planets at the time of one's birth.

In knowing your birth chart, you can uncover what type of activities and work come naturally to you. It can also show you what you need to work on more.

Knowing your natal chart can help you understand what types of experiences shape you into a stronger person, and what people and places you should avoid.

Once you begin to feel more empowered on your journey the more confident you become in reading your own sign because after all, no one else can really do all this work for you. No one else should be able to tell you how to think, feel, or love.

Dear souls,

It gave us great pleasure to have been able to co create this book for you. We hope you find it enlightening and also helpful on your own spiritual path. This beginners guide really is setting the foundation for letting the Consciousness of Christ into your hearts.

We know and understand how oftentimes it can feel sad and lonely on this journey. So, we want you to understand, You cannot have the perfect spiritual partner in your life until you yourself becomes the perfect spiritual partner. We are all growing together in love. Relax in knowing, as you heal, so will your divine counterpart. As you are divinely connected.

It is important now more than ever for you to stand firm in your beliefs. That is simply why you are here. Do not continue to let the negative forces in this world win. Be uniquely you.

Divinely Sarah

Abundance: In a spiritual context, the notion of abundance or plenty is less about material conditions, revolving instead (once basic needs are met), around an appreciation of life in its fullness, joy and strength of mind, body and soul. This is the cultivation of respect for the creative energy of the universe.

Ascension: the act of rising or ascending especially : the act of moving to a higher or more powerful position.

Akashic Records: is a compendium of all universal events, thoughts, words, emotions, and intent ever to have occurred in the past, present, or future in terms of all entities and life forms, not just human. They are believed by theosophists to be encoded in a non-physical plane of existence known as the mental plane. It is believed all thoughts, words, intent etc. generates its own unique "frequency or vibration" which is stored in the Akashic Records

Alienated: to cause to be estranged : to make unfriendly, hostile, or indifferent especially where attachment formerly existed

Astral Plane: also called the astral realm or the astral world, is a plane of existence postulated by classical, medieval, oriental, and esoteric philosophies and mystery religions.

Awakening: coming into existence or awareness.

Bondage: the state of being a slave.

Boundaries: a line that marks the limits of an area; a dividing line.

Chakras: In Sanskrit, the word "chakra" means "disk" or "wheel" and refers to the energy centers in your body. These wheels or disks of spinning energy each correspond to certain nerve bundles and major organs.

Christ: person who is conscious of their behavior and actions. A person who can give/receive love and compassion without wanting anything back in return. individuals that can demonstrate and project the attributes of unconditional love and compassion consciously through their thoughts, actions, and behaviors.

Christ's Consciousness: means a person who embraces and demonstrates divinity. individuals that can demonstrate and project the attributes of unconditional love and compassion consciously through their thoughts, actions, and behaviors.

Compassion: sympathetic pity and concern for the sufferings or misfortunes of others.

Compensation: something, typically money, awarded to someone as a recompense for loss, injury, or suffering.

Conscious: 1 : capable of or marked by thought, will, design, or perception : relating to, being, or being part of consciousness the conscious mind conscious and unconscious processes. 2 : having mental faculties undulled by sleep, faintness, or stupor became conscious after the anesthesia wore off.

Correspondence: a close similarity, connection, or equivalence

Detox: abstain from or rid the body of toxic or unhealthy substancesAbundance

Divine: of, from, or like God or a god.

Divine Person: individual that can demonstrate and project the attributes of unconditional love and compassion consciously through their thoughts, actions, and behaviors.

Divinity: the highest characteristics, personal qualities of the absolute divine

Dysfunctional Relationships: Dysfunctional Relationships are relationships that do not perform their appropriate function; that is, they do not emotionally support the participants, foster communication among them, appropriately challenge them, or prepare or fortify them for life in the larger world.

Emotional Wounds: a deep hurt, pain, or fear caused by separation from someone else who is a source of security and safety that over time results in internal and external expressions of anger, frustration, resentment, hatred, and guilt.

Empathy: the ability to understand and share the feelings of another.

Enlightenment: has become synonymous with self-realization and the true self and false self, being regarded as a substantial essence being covered over by social conditioning.

Etheric: is of or relating to the ether as a physical medium.

Etheric World: to represent the subtle part of the lower plane of existence. It represents the fourth [higher] subplane of the physical plane (a hyperplane), the lower three being the states of solid, liquid, and gaseous matter.

Gypsy: a member of a people originating in South Asia and traditionally having an itinerant way of life, living widely dispersed across Europe and North and South America and speaking a language (Romani) that is related to Hindi; a Romani person.

Ignorance: lack of knowledge or information.

Integrate: combine (one thing) with another so that they become a whole

Joy: a feeling of great pleasure and happiness.

Love: an intense feeling of deep affection.

Oneness: the fact or state of being one in number.

Peace: freedom from disturbance; tranquility.

Permeates: spread throughout (something); pervade.

Perpetual: occurring repeatedly; so frequent as to seem endless and uninterrupted

Qualified: make (someone) competent or knowledgeable enough to do something.

Raptured: (according to some millenarian teaching) the transporting of believers to heaven at the Second Coming of Christ.

Religion: a particular system of faith and worship.

Scrutiny: critical observation or examination.

Self Care: the practice of taking an active role in protecting one's own well-being and happiness, in particular during periods of stress.

Spiritual: relating to or affecting the human spirit or soul as opposed to material or physical things.

Star Seed: Star people (New Age belief), individuals who believe they originated from another world or planet.

Synchronicity: the simultaneous occurrence of events which appear significantly related but have no discernible causal connection.

Taboo: a social or religious custom prohibiting or forbidding discussion of a particular practice or forbidding association with a particular person, place, or thing.

Telepathically: direct transference of thought from one person (sender or agent) to another (receiver or recipient) without using the usual sensory channels of communication, hence a form of extrasensory perception (ESP).

Toleration: the practice of tolerating something, in particular differences of opinion or behavior.

Transform: make a thorough or dramatic change in the form, appearance, or character of.

Unconditional Love: is known as affection without any limitations, or love without conditions. This term is sometimes associated with other terms such as true altruism or complete love. Each area of expertise has a certain way of describing unconditional love, but most will agree that it is that type of love which has no bounds and is unchanging.

Unity: the state of being united or joined as a whole.

Vibrational Changes: experts claim that certain emotions and thought patterns, such as joy, peace, and acceptance, create high frequency vibrations, while other feelings and mindsets (such as anger, despair, and fear) vibrate at a lower rate.

Work: activity involving mental or physical effort done in order to achieve a purpose or result.

About the Author

───────── ❖ ─────────

Sarah enjoys filling her days with Spirit and teaching her children from home. She has a fluffy fat cat named Manfred. Avid lover of animals, rocks, plants, and art! Sarah is learning to find great joy in navigating life's difficult waves for and with her tribe. She finds that to be the most fulfilling part. More importantly, at one time Sarah was just like you. Looking for something better, knowing there had to be more, and stopping at nothing to find it.

Printed in the United States
by Baker & Taylor Publisher Services